Sparks Fly Upward

Sparks Fly Upward
Text Copyright © 2017 by Katie Spivey Brewster

The use of the brand name Irish Spring is not endorsed by Colgate-Palmolive.

For information address:

J2B Publishing LLC
4251 Columbia Park Road
Pomfret, MD 20675
www.J2BLLC.com
GladToDoIt@gmail.com

Printed and bound in the United States of America.
This book is set in Garamond. Designed by Mary Barrows.

ISBN: 978-1-941927-55-7- Paperback
      978-1-941927-56-4- Hardback

Sparks Fly Upward

By **Katie Brewster**

J2B PUBLISHING

~ Dedication ~

With admiration, love, and gratitude, I dedicate
this collection of poems to my mother,

Laura Keith Spivey

Table of Contents

I - Poems

13	My Daddy's Legacy
15	Sparks Fly Upward
17	Sensory Seashore
19	Where, Oh Where?
21	Candle Prompts
23	A Lady of Books
25	Walls
27	Ice Prompts
29	Pretty Apricot
31	Summer Garden Reverie
33	Watering Flowers
35	Bird Bath (ing)
37	"Global Warming"
39	With Dawn's Blush
41	Tuesday Doings
43	Elusive Irish Spring
45	Friday and Feeling Fine
47	Saturday Sights
49	Thank you, Dear Note Pad
51	The Prince of Andalusia
53	Morning Walk

II - Acrostics

57	Smile
59	I-Phone
61	Gratitude (Privilege/Duty)
63	Tigger
65	Frenetically Exhausted
67	Teacher
69	Sandy Cove
71	Crab
73	Capt Billy
75	Butter
77	Tsondoku
79	Benjamin Yates Brewster
81	Rose of Sharon
83	Ode to Sky Mall

III - Haiku

89	Three Heliotrope Haiku
91	Two Azure Haiku
93	Two Tea Haiku and a Punchy Third
95	Vermillion

IV - Cinquain

101	Hammock
101	Cinquain
101	Website
103	Tweetspeak
103	Walking

V - I Am From

107	I am From

8

Introduction

I like reading poetry.
Poetry can be fun, creative, serious, uplifting – and it gives us a voice in our darkest times.

I like writing poetry.
Poetry is having fun with words; it is making them dance, play, and sing.

This past year, Tweet Speak Poetry (*www.tweetspeakpoetry.com*) watered my serious interest in writing poetry through its blog posts that taught me how to write poetry, gave me prompts so I would actually write, and encouraged me through their comments about my poems.

In fact, most of the poems in *Sparks Fly Upward* were inspired by Tweet Speak Poetry (TSP) prompts. For example, the Poetry Prompt theme for August was "Flying Machines," with week one being, "The Great Kite," followed by "Ode to Sky Mall," then "Animate" and the last week as "Wing Envy." Ode to Sky Mall caught my interest, and since I was enjoying acrostics at the time, I took a crack at it that way.

I also found three books that were extremely helpful in fanning my poetry interest:

> *How to Read a Poem* – Tania Runyan
> *How to Write a Poem* - Tania Runyan
> *The Joy of Poetry* – Megan Willome

So, come join the fun and let your poetry plant grow.

I

Poems

My Daddy's Legacy

Houston Lee Spivey (1924 - 2008)

Saturday night prep
for Sunday morn:
bath, shoeshine, lesson -

read and studied,
equipped to give an answer,
to share the hope within.

Spoken or lived:
whether throwing horse shoes,
mixing mortar, laying brick -

upon brick, to build a house
to shelter his family
so they may weather any storm.

Written 6/21/16 to a TSP prompt to write a tribute poem.

6/23/16 - This explanation written in response to TSP reader comments. "I love to honor my father's memory as he gave and meant so much for me and my sibs. He definitely had a servant's heart, always looking to help family and contribute to his community."

Sparks Fly Upward

Vertical shooting stars
zigzag into a darkening sky

Faces glowing, eyes sparkling
follow as they soar high

Bonfire popping and crackling
sends grains of light up

To dance on the evening breeze
swirling and twirling above

Craning our necks
we follow their flight

Disappearing over tree tops
Well out of sight –

but not out of mind.

Sensory Seashore

One must have a mind of summer
to see the shimmer of heat over pavement
like hot waves above a grill.

To smell the salt laden breeze
as the bridge comes into view
knowing the island, shore and ocean, lie just beyond.

To hear the foamy splash
slap onto the beach
chilling ankles, making toes pruney.

To feel the prickle of gooseflesh
upon arms and shoulders
as the swells recede.

To taste the salty spray,
when waves break over your head
running down your face into your laughing mouth.

where, Oh where?

As I tumble toward the ground
I wonder where I will
be found.

Will I be put in a hard-packed sphere –
part of a snowball fight this year?

Or be on this day
in a snow bank
along a highway?

Will I be blown by the wind
into a snow fence with my kin?

Or be part of the biggest this winter,
the largest snowfall
seen in many a year?

Will I be taken for a ride down hill
on a ziggy-zagging snowmobile?

Or be scooped up now
by a lumbering
snowplow?

Will I be worn for a second or two
on a little child's cold snowsuit?

Or just be – "Oh pooh,"
stepped on by
her daddy's snowshoe?

Where ever I land, I'm sure it will have been
an interesting journey until the end.

Had fun writing this playful poem for the TSP prompt "Snowflake"

Candle Prompt

String in
wax

Match to
string

Flame of
light

Piercing
night

Wax drips
down

Smoke wafts
up

Ceiling shadow
bouncing 'round.

A Lady of Books

There once was a lady of books.
She looked and she looked and she looked.
But she couldn't find any good reads,
None at all to meet her needs.
So a bookless vacation she took.

My family teases me that I look like a "bag lady" wherever I go —
trip or not — due to my ever-present tote bag(s) of books. Actually, it
would be highly unusual for me not to find any good reads whether I'm
searching the library, a bookstore, or just my own bookshelves!

Walls

I can enclose
as did The Great Wall,
an entire country.

I can divide
as did the Berlin Wall,
east and west.

I can support
as did sea walls,
the shore along the gulf.

I can provide
as does the sound barrier wall,
between beltway and city.

I can protect
keep from harm or injury
as does a border wall.

Ice Prompt

ice cap >
ice pack >
ice field >
ice floe >
ice berg > T
                I
                    T
                        A
                            N
                                I
                                    C

Pretty Apricots

You smiled up at my appetite,
from the cylinder
in the salad bar.

Small halves of sunshine,
wet and shiny
mouth-watering.

Wooing me to spoon
you onto my plate
as I smile and drool.

This summer I was so happy that apricots had been added to the fruit section of the salad bar in the dining hall at Sandy Cove.

Summer Garden Reverie

Bumble bees crawl over blossoms

Butterflies skip and dip flower to flower

Collection of colors

Compilation of motions

Delightful days

Delicious ways, of seeing

When butterflies and bumble bees visit the plants while I'm watering or weeding, I stop and watch them, marveling at their flight and industry.

Watering Flowers

Gather green spouted cans
Hold under faucet
Fill with life-giving fluid.

Round the yard
Visit beds of impatiens
reach hanging petunias.

Pour wetness
gently reviving blooms
nourishing stems, leaves

Step back
Gaze on beauty
Color, shape, texture.

This poem sounds a little like a recipe or instruction manual, but for me it's the sequence I enjoy as I tend my garden.

Flower gardening is more than enjoyable or fun for me. It is soothing and therapeutic. I'm so grateful to the Creator for the colors, shapes, variety, aromas, and textures, and for the senses to take them in.

When it rains so much that watering isn't necessary, I miss its rhythm.

Bird Bath (ing)

From the screened-in porch
we watch(ed) them come.

Some flitting,
Others swooping or diving
Dropping down, jumping up
Branches bobbing.

Splashing, ducking
then shaking
Now they preen
before taking wing.

A favorite pastime at "The Spivey Nest" (as my family often refers to my mother's house) is sitting together on the back porch, watching birds come and go as they visit the feeders and birdbath.

"Global Warming"

Let's see -
the blizzard of '10
took out the azalea by the garage.

Then, I think it
was the ice storm
last winter that brought down
the leaning pine.

Must have been
year before last
the Maxwell's metal carport
caved in to record snowfall.

Hmmm - so that's why some folks joke about Global Warming, I suppose.

With Dawn's Blush

With dawn's blush

    the trees were awash

        with colors lavish.

Tuesday Doings

Towels in washer
Potted sweet potato vines
Gentle breeze, rustling leaves
Hanging baskets next.

Shaded potting bench
Sunny flower beds
Birds sing from branches above
Crickets in surround sound hum.

Weeding done
Potting soil down
All plants watered
Time to make supper.

I've found I need to do some housekeeping before going outside, so I often put a load of laundry in before beginning in the garden. Some days, when I've gotten on a roll and don't want to come in, supper can end up being rather late. If this poem were to carry a post script it would read, "I'm thankful for our picnic table which allows me to extend my time in the yard and share a meal out of doors with the family."

Elusive Irish Spring©

Slip-sliding
Out of my fingers
All the way
Past my toes

Swirl-twirling
Under my
Drenched
Sudsy self . . . it g - o - e - s !

Written in response to the TSP "Thank You Note to Soap" poetry prompt.

Friday and Feeling Fine

Summer breeze:
>Sways wind chimes
>rustles tree leaves
>billows laundry
>on the clothesline
>
>Tousles hair
>wiggles flower blossoms
>bounces magnolia blooms
>heavy with sweet nectar
>
>Clouds drift above
>tree tops
>gaps of blue peek
>through

Sunshine:
>grows plantings
>in tandem
>with the water from
>the gardener's can
>
>Peaches ripen on the
>window sill
>smell of sweetness
>foretells cobbler's delight

In addition to gardening, I also enjoy baking, and cobbler is one of my favorite desserts. Just as very ripe bananas make yummy bread or muffins, well-ripened peaches produce delicious cobbler.

Saturday Sights

Neale Sound
Cobb Island
Ospreys in flight

Dark clouds
Bright white clouds
Shoreline in sight

Soybean fields
Corn fields
Yield yet, they might

Nature is good for us to experience, because God hard-wired us to like blues and greens — all colors really — but the sky and land and sea He gave us in particular to be a balm to our soul.

Thank You, Dear Notepad

Dear Notepad,

Thank you for reminding me to:

call Beverly

get paper towels

schedule my mammogram

reschedule dentist appointment for Sam

fwd Ann Voskamp post to Karen

send Tigger an e-mail message

shop with Rachel for shoes

text that picture to Pat

write a grocery list

write a thank you note to Sue & Ted

go to the P. O.

get gas at WAWA

get cash from the ATM

make the deposit at NFCU

go to Gina's

check the LFL's to see if they need more books (kids/adults)

return library books and CDs to CCPL

try the latest TSP prompt :)

The Prince of Andalusia

You spectacular bird
peafowl, peacock
makes no difference
where you flock

preening yourself
for all to see
right under our noses
pretty as you please

you strut and stride
'cross the yard
with all that pride
for nothin's too hard

when you're plucky
and sprite
you always feel lucky
though never in flight

forward and backward
dancing, you go
backward and forward
surely and slow.

Morning Walk

Sunlight slants through
    towering poplars.

Doves coo gently
    above on the wire.

Red berries hang
    low on a limb.

Hawk lifts swiftly
    off the ground.

Soft breeze stirs
    feathery Mimosa blooms.

Dew drops glisten
    atop blades of grass.

Pedestrian footfalls
    eyes and ears alert.

Azure sky domes
    over us all.

II

Acrostics

S M I L E

Sweet expression

Mouth held right

I love to see these

Laughing outright

Effervescent emotion

I like acrostics because they require you to be very precise in your thinking while at the same time giving you the flexibility to use a phrase instead of just one word.

I P H O N E

I put it down

Pick it up

Habitual

Over and over

Not

Even knowing why

GRATITUDE
Privilege/Duty

Get to

Rather than have to

Always the

True

Insight

That helps

Us

Discern what is of

Excellent Worth

61

TIGGER

Total energizer

Incorrigible pest

Grumpy as all get out

Going against the grain

Encourager extraordinaire

Ridiculously fun

Tigger is a nickname I have for a loved one.

FRENTICALLY EXHAUSTED

Faster, faster

Run, run, run

Everything

Needs to be done.

Even if I'm out of energy

Tired, too bad

I can't stop

Cause

All these tasks

Literally

Logically

Yell at me until I drop.

E-v-e-r-y-thing

X/Y/Z

Has to be

Accomplished

Under

Strict

Total

Endless

Duress

This is how I felt during many of our parenting and home schooling years while teaching and raising our children. At times, I thought all the extra-curricular activities would be the death of me (Scouts - mtgs, campouts, fundraisers, etc; Baseball and Soccer - practices, games, fundraisers, snacks ...)

TEACHER

Trainer

Educator

And

Curiosity

Harbinger

Empower-er

Re-molder

While I often felt overwhelmed by the mission at the time, I was nevertheless grateful we had the privilege of educating our children and as time passes and our children make their contributions to the world, my gratitude has only increased. I am so proud of each of them.

SANDY COVE

Summer of sunshine on water

A green lawn slopes to shore

Now dotted with pairs of wooden Adirondack chairs

Dock has watercraft tied along ramp

Yearning to be ridden again

Comers all are offered His rest

Openly giving some of His best

Variety of refreshment

Even sleep, sweet sleep

Sandy Cove Conference and Retreat Center in North East, Maryland holds a special place in my heart. It has been a haven of rest and a place of rejuvenation for me and has ministered to our family since 2000. I wrote this acrostic during a poetry workshop there in June of 2017. Each attendee wrote a Sandy Cove poem. What a joy to hear how Sandy Cove blessed each person.

CRAB

Crustaceans

Really messy

All hands on deck

Bring wipes.

CAPT BILLY

Crabs

All Maryland

Patience Required

Totally messy

Bring your appetite

Is not instant gratification

Lick your fingers

Love Old Bay

Yesiree Billy

Created 7/2/17 at Capt Billy's while picking crabs with my daughter, Rachel, and my husband, Jim. Wrote Crabs and Capt Billy on a napkin while waiting for Jim and Rachel to finish their crab claws.

BUTTER

Butter comes from milk

Utterly smooth as silk

Tempting me

Teasing me

Every pat pleasing me

Right – you know their ilk

This was written in response to another fun prompt on TSP.

TSONDOKU

Japanese - accumulating books, but not reading them

Totally

Sold

Out

Nearly

Dependent

On

Knowledge

Unlimited

(LEAVE PILED UP – is the root meaning of tsondoku)

Let me get this book

Even though I know it looks

As if I'll never stop

Veering into bookshops

Eager to acquire one more.

Please will you hold the door?

I need just one more

Last set of book

Ends for my

Den's bookshelves that are spilling onto the floor.

Unless, you know, this is just another false

Pledge

BENJAMIN YATES BREWSTER
(My father-in-law 1928 - 2016)

Believable

Engaging, excellent flautist

Natural musician, Native New Englander

Jovial

Aboveboard agent

Multi-talented

Insightful

Namesake

Yachtsman, Yates

Accomplished pianist

Terrific Poppa

Erudite

Sanguine shipmate - cheerfully confident, optimistic

Bilingual Brewster

Reasonable, racer of sailboats

Eloquent, elderly, executive

Wholehearted - earnest commitment, sincerity and enthusiasm

Savvy crossword puzzler, self-effacing

Thoughtful, tidy, team player

Engaging

Raconteur - accomplished and witty storyteller

ROSE OF SHARON

Regal

Opulent

Sensational

Every bloom a blessing

Open

Faces

Show

Hues

And

Ruffles

Of

Natural beauty

The initial residents of our house planted Rose of Sharon. Their plants have bloomed more profusely this summer than ever. We have reaped the visual harvest of their labor.

Ode to S KY MALL

Selling
Krap
Yanking my attention from the flight attendant

Materialism
American-style
Lots and
Lots of stuff, plenty of stuff!

Store in the air
Krazy products
Yep

Money required
American Express or
Loads and
Loads of cash!

The TSP prompt theme for August was "Flying Machines." Home and family kept me from writing to "The Great Kite" or "Animate," but I had time when "Ode to Sky Mall" caught my interest. Since I was enjoying acrostics at the time, I took a crack at it that way.

III

Haiku

Haiku

Haiku (Hi Coo) is a traditional Japanese form of poetry comprised of three lines totaling seventeen syllables, written in a 5/7/5 syllable count. Haiku require a poet to focus on simplicity, intensity, and directness of expression. Nature is often a subject of Haiku.

The philosophy of haiku is to focus on a brief moment in time; use provocative, colorful images; create a sense of sudden enlightenment and illumination; and be able to be read in one breath.

Three Heliotrope Haiku

Old, old helio
So pretty on countess gown
Or Bertie's PJs

Lovely, helio
we've seen you every-where
Luggage to pencils

Widow half-mourning
Dons heliotrope clothing
Good Victorian

Wikipedia was a good source of information for this. There I learned quite a bit about this color.

Two Azure Haiku

opaque azure-blue
to deep blue, used as a
gemstone; lazurite

a light purplish blue
pretty, semi-precious stone
azure blue, opaque

Two Tea Haiku and a Punchy Third

jasmine green hot tea
sofa and chairs by the fire
scone, Nutella, yum

coffee regulars
sit around sipping the joe
tease the newcomer

Dragon well – will it?
Will it make my dragon well?
Yes, if her draft's long ;)

One TSP post described LaBella, a tea/coffee shop that sounded like my kind of place. It had a fireplace, lovely cabinet/hutch with tea tins, a pretty "Each day is a Fresh Start" chalkboard, and then a delicious menu including Nutella and hot oatmeal. Oh my goodness, sign me up!

Vermillion

From antiquity
you have decorated skin,
paintings, clothes, dishes

Yesterday, my dear hubby gave me a copy of A is for Azure, an alphabet book based upon colors. It's beautiful, colorful, and lovely:):):). Then today's TSP's poetry prompt was on the color vermilion. What came to mind was this Haiku

IV

Cinquain

Cinquain

A cinquain (Sin Cane) is a "form poem" meaning in creating the poem the poet must conform to a strict structure. In the case of a cinquain, the poet is limited to 22 syllables which must be organized into five lines in a 2/4/6/8/2 pattern. For many, the Japanese Haiku comes to mind.

The cinquain was made popular in America by Adelaide Crapsey in the early 1900s. Her cinquain's demonstrated that five lines and 22 syllables provides ample room to tell a complete story.

The stories in Adelaide's cinquains revealed themselves in this order.
1st line: (2 syllables) Subject.
2nd line: (4 syllables) Describe it.
3rd line: (6 syllables) Include an action.
4th line: (8 syllables) Add feelings.
5th line: (2 syllables) Conclusion.

I found the cinquain to be both challenging and enjoyable. It is challenging to have to "stay within the lines" of the cinquain but extremely enjoyable to discover how much can be said and effectively convey within 22 syllables and five lines.

Hammock

hammock
sleep inducer
swaying from side to side
lazily swinging, so soothing
naptime

Cinquain

cinquain
Adelaide's gift
her spirit the artist's
let us remember and honor
her craft

Website

website
for word lovers
writing new poetry
which laughs/lends/lifts/longs/lilts/lures/lasts
loves life

Tweetspeak

Tweetspeak
word lovers play
we sing, we dance, we cry
or we whisper, or shout, or moan
Sharing.

Walking

Walking
the neighborhood
early of a morning
comings and goings, waving "hi"
or "bye"

V

I Am From

I Am From

I am from iced tea,
From Ajax and Lysol.
I am from the lot by the creek
Clean, tidy, smelling of Pine Sol,
I am from Azaleas and Dogwoods beautiful and handsome
I'm from pot luck dinners and camping trips
From Houston Lee and Annie Laura
I'm from obsessive compulsive disorder and perfectionism, "if you
can't say something nice, don't say anything at all."
From don't do a thing halfway.
I'm from the Southern Baptist Convention, the Wilmington
Association to be specific.
I'm from Waverly, OH and the Spivey and Keith Clans.
Cherry Yum-Yum, Congo squares
From the couple who eloped and stayed married 61 years.
The bricklayer and the seamstress
pictures and scrap books in drawers recording many a happy time.

*I Am From was written using a template posted by Michelle DeRusha
on her Everyday faith. Faith Every Day blog. The template is on the
next page. Now you write your own.*

I Am From Poem
Use this template to draft your poem, and then write a final draft to share on blank paper.

I am from _____
          (specific ordinary item)

From _____ and _____
      (product name)   (product name)

I am from the _____
              (home description)

_____ , _____ , _____
(adjective)   (adjective)   (sensory detail)

I am from _____ ,
        (plant, flower, natural item)

_____
     (description of above item)

I'm from _____ and _____
      (family tradition)   (family trait)

From _____ and _____
    (name of family member)   (another family name)

I'm from the _____ and _____
     (description of family tendency) (another one)

From _____ and _____
   (something you were told as a child)   (another)

I'm from _____ , _____
   (representation of religion or lack of), (further description)

I'm from _____
     (place of birth and family ancestry)

_____ , _____
(a food item that represents your family)   (another one)

From the _____
    (specific family story about a specific person and detail)

Meet the Author

Katie Spivey Brewster was raised in Wilmington, NC, learned to body surf at Wrightsville Beach, married Jim Brewster from Slingerlands, NY, and raised and home schooled five children (Ben, Luke, Rachel, Andrew, and Sam). She is the author of *Feast of Memories* and of *Aunt Louise Comes to Visit* - a story in rhyme. She is currently Nana to five grandchildren (Levi, Micah, Judah, Felicity, and Seth).

www.ingramcontent.com/pod-product-compliance
Lightning Source LLC
Chambersburg PA
CBHW071614040426
42452CB00008B/1339